PRÜFUNGSTEXTE

FÜR DIE FREMDSPRACHLICHE WIRTSCHAFTS-KORRESPONDENTENPRÜFUNG

ENGLISCH

Fachverlag Th. Grossmann
7000 Stuttgart 50
Ebitzweg 18

Zusammengestellt von Hilda Th. Freyd-Wadham, Lektorin

Vorwort

Dieses Buch hat den Zweck, einen Überblick über die Prüffächer der fremdsprachlichen Korrespondent(innen)prüfung zu geben und zugleich durch die Darbietung von 10 Aufgaben je Fach die Grundlage für eine methodische Vorbereitung auf diese Prüfung zu ermöglichen.

Die Sammlung umfaßt die Prüfungsaufgaben der vom Kultusministerium Baden-Württemberg in den letzten Jahren durchgeführten staatlichen Wirtschaftskorrespondentenprüfungen im Englischen (Prüfungsplan s. Seite 4), deren Grundschema im allgemeinen demjenigen der anderen im deutschen Sprachraum abgehaltenen Auslandskorrespondentenprüfung entsprechen dürfte.

3. Auflage: 1982 mit den neusten Prüfungstexten bis Herbst 1981

ISBN 3-87217-160-7

INHALT

Schriftliche Prüfung

I	Englische Diktate	5 - 16
II	Übersetzung von Geschäftsbriefen ins Englische	17 - 28
III	Übersetzung von Wirtschaftstexten ins Deutsche	29 - 40
IV	Aufsatzthemen	41 - 43
V	Anfertigen von Geschäftsbriefserien in Englisch	49 - 59

Mündliche Prüfung

Übersetzungstexte (Prima-Vista-Texte)　　　　　61 - 71

Prüfungsplan

A. Schriftliche Prüfung

a) Fremdsprachliches Diktat. Text wirtschaftlichen Inhalts von etwa 300 Wörtern.

b) Übersetzung eines Geschäftsbriefs aus dem Deutschen in die Fremdsprache, insgesamt etwa 280 Wörter; Zeit: 100 Minuten.

c) Übersetzung aus der Fremdsprache ins Deutsche, Text wirtschaftlichen Inhalts. Umfang etwa 250 Wörter; Zeit: 90 Minuten.

d) Aufsatz über ein Thema aus dem Wirtschaftsleben (3 Themen zur Wahl); Zeit: 2 Stunden.

e) Anfertigung einer Serie von Geschäftsbriefen in der Fremdsprache nach Skizzierung des betreffenden geschäftlichen Vorgangs in deutscher Sprache; Zeit: 2 Stunden.

Die Benützung von Hilfsmitteln ist nicht zugelassen.
Die schriftliche Prüfung findet an 2 Tagen hintereinander statt.

B. Mündliche Prüfung

1. Lesen und Übersetzen eines fremdsprachlichen Textes wirtschaftlichen Inhalts (10 - 15 Minuten).

2. Behandlung von Grundfragen des kaufmännischen Lebens in der Fremdsprache (10 - 15 Minuten). *)

*) Anmerkung: Es werden jeweils zum Zeitpunkt der Prüfung akutelle Themen behandelt. Zur Vorbereitung empfiehlt sich das Lesen von Artikeln aus Wirtschaftszeitungen, wie z.B. "The Economist." Ferner wird auf die auf Seite 72 dieses Buches aufgeführten Lehrbücher zur Vorbereitung auf die Prüfungen hingewiesen.

Schriftliche Prüfung

I
Englisches Diktat

U.S. corporate lawyers face competition

U.S. corporate law practice is undergoing deep and rapid change. The 1970s were a decade of great growth, expansion and prosperity for U.S. large law firms. Most expanded internally at a rate in excess of ten per cent per year. Many opened additional offices domestically and abroad.

This rapid growth appears finally to be slowing down. Some quantum surges in company size are still occurring, but they are now resulting less from internal expansion than from mergers, often to establish multiple offices in different regions. However, while growth is slowing down, changes in the nature of practice are accelerating.

Perhaps the most fundamental change is that U.S. lawyers will encounter more competition than ever before. That is likely to reduce profitability, slow growth even further, and lead to the development of even more highly specialised expertise offered by individual firms as they seek to differentiate their services from competitors and meet the constantly changing needs of their clients.

The new competitiveness is the result of several factors. First law firms are having increasing difficulty controlling costs of operation. This is most evident in recruiting attorneys. Salaries for young lawyers have increased dramatically in the past 15 years. Competition for the best students leads to the hiring of full-time recruitment administrators and travel and entertainment budgets of many thousands of dollars.

Secondly, traditional Washington law firms, for example, no longer have the partial advantage of proximity to the federal governmental process. Similarly, New York law firms used to have a near-monopoly of major corporate financial representation.

Since no firm can have equally outstanding competence in every area of law, there is an emerging tendency to accentuate specialised expertise. Illustrating this, small firms have proliferated representing only a few large clients in one or two highly specialised fields of law such as trade, environment or white-collar crime.

The Affluent Society

Wealth is not without its advantages and the case to the contrary, although is has often been made, has never proved widely persuasive.

The experience of nations with well-being is exceedingly brief. Nearly all, throughout all history, have been very poor. The exception, almost insignificant in the whole span of human existence, has been the last few generations in the comparatively small corner of the world populated by Europeans. Here, and especially in the United States, there has been great and quite unprecedented affluence.

The ideas by which these people interpret their existence, and in measure guide their behaviour, were not forged in a world of wealth. These ideas were the product of a world in which poverty had always been man's normal lot, and any other state was in degree unimaginable. This poverty was not the elegant torture of the spirit which comes from contemplating another man's more spacious possessions. It was the unedifying mortification of the flesh - from hunger, sickness, and cold. Those who might be freed temporarily from such burden could not know when it would strike again, for at best hunger yielded only perilously to privation.

No one would wish to argue that the ideas which interpreted this world of grim scarcity would serve equally well for the contemporary United States. Poverty was the all-persuasive fact of that world. Obviously it is not of ours. One would not expect that the preoccupations of a poverty-ridden world would be relevant in one where the ordinary individual has access to amenities - foods, entertainment, personal transportation, and plumbing - in which not even the rich rejoiced a century ago. So great has been the change that many of the desires of the individual are not longer evident to him. They become so only as they are synthesized, elaborated, and nurtured by advertising and salesmanship.

Reading the tea leaves

Has the British economic miracle at last arrived? The pound is rising, the current account is in surplus, the rate of price inflation is the lowest for 5 years and personal consumption is at record levels. It is a measure of the erosion of national self-confidence, or perhaps just realism, that no one is now talking about a dash for growth. Even the bland statements on the economy in the Commons last week by the Prime Minister and the Chancellor of the Exchequer were relatively low key, and industry has been distinctly cautious about the extent of the upturn.

Although the Government itself has been noticeably reticent about the prospects for the next 12 months, there is a surprising degree of unanimity in the batch of forecasts and analyses produced in the past week. The agreed view is that the growth of both disposable incomes and output will slow down significantly from the end of the year onwards with the rate of price inflation hovering around 10 per cent.

But the faithless do not have to put their trust solely in forecasts; there are clear enough signs in what is happening now to the economy. There are two main guides which have proved reliable in recent years — the real money supply and the Central Statistical Office's index of longer leading indicators.

The significance of the real money supply has been highlighted in particular by the London Business School. In the last couple of years, fluctuations of the real money stock have accurately foreshadowed by a few months turning-points in economic activity. For example, it became clear that domestic spending would start rising rapidly this spring and summer following the turnround from a sharply declining real rate of monetary expansion in early 1977 to an annual growth rate of over 17 per cent by early 1978.

Afloat, but can they moor it?

Mr. Healey has done on Monday what he felt unable to do only last Wednesday. Under the pressure of relentlessly accumulating inflows of money, on a scale which increasingly jeopardised his monetary targets, he has set the pound free, aiming to let it float up which was not precisely stated yesterday. The test of what he has done will be how far this upward float continues. If it can be held to a relatively modest appreciation — say five per cent, or perhaps a shade more — then the move may well pay off; there will be useful gains in the form of mitigating inflation, while the losses, in Britain's diminished competitiveness in overseas markets, will at least be reasonably containable. If the float gets out of hand — and ominously the markets yesterday were talking in terms of anything up to a two dollar pound — the consequences could be extremely dangerous: exports would be crippled, unemployment would grow, and the new bumper pound would be permanently vulnerable to a fresh speculative attack.

So the wisdom of what Mr. Healey has done can in this sense only be judged by results. What can be said even now, however, is that the move he made yesterday fits very oddly with the strategy on which last week's mini-budget was apparently based. As we said then, a forecast for the public sector borrowing requirement which falls more than £ 1 billion below what the IMF was happy to accept means that Mr. Healey is now presiding over a measure of deflation even more savage than that over which the Cabinet wrangled so bitterly years ago — and wholly out of keeping with the Government's professed desire to get Britain back on the road to growth and fuller employment.

Swiss Tighten Bank Secrecy Rules

In an unprecedented and wide-ranging commitment, Swiss banks have agreed to prevent abuse of this country's famed secrecy laws, to avoid aiding and abetting illegal transfer and to abstain from helping clients who seek to deceive tax authorities at home or abroad. The Swiss National Bank president said the pact with the Swiss Bankers' Association is an immediate consequence of the Chiasso affair, in which the management of a bank branch on the Italian border allegedly misdirected huge funds and now stands to lose 1 billion francs.
Though it would not rule out another scandal, the pact would reduce the chances of such a recurrence.
A small decline in the value of the Swiss franc (if capital inflows slowed and outflows increased) because of these restrictions was definitely to be foreseen.
The new restrictions apply to Swiss numbered accounts and a joint communiqué issued by the two sides said that this problem had been eased significantly.
The agreement codified behaviour that has always been observed by an overwhelming majority of banks; and it is expected that the others will also accede to the pact.
The joint communiqué said that the purpose of the pact was to vouchsafe that the identity of the banks' clients is reliably ascertained, implicitly to prevent tax evasion and the acceptance of funds recognised to be acquired by punishable acts.
A significant article of the agreement requires banks to terminate relations with clients if information concerning the beneficial owner is suspect, or if improper acts are performed through the bank by a client.
The agreement establishes sanctions for banks that violate the pact. In cases of violation the bank will be fined up to 10 million francs. To ascertain and punish offences, an arbitration committee will be established, comprised of two representatives of the central bank and two of the Bankers' Association, chaired by a federal judge unanimously designated by the committee members.

The First Days

Nothing, of course, has been irretrievably committed in these days, but President Carter's sketch of an agenda is bold, even venturesome. Too much can be made of his slow and steady cadence, the symbolic gestures to down-home simplicity. There is no telling how the new President will fare, but he is leaving a trail of clues about what he will attempt: a lot.

He wants to stimulate the economy and inspire confidence in investors and consumers while also hoarding the revenues that will let him mount major federal programs to deal with unemployment, welfare and health care. He wants to devise an energy program that will conserve resources at home and regain bargaining leverage abroad.

There is more than that in Mr. Carter's campaign litany of promises and objectives, but these objectives have already passed from the speech writers to the new team of administrators and emissaries. The style is still exploratory, reinforcing the campaign image of a prudent man who can be stared down into quick compromise. But the appetite looks large.

The best evidence lies in Mr. Carter's proposed stimulus for the economy. Conservatives wished for a permanent tax cut, to be spent randomly in response to market forces. Liberals wished for accelerated programs of job creation. Mr. Carter decided upon $31 billion, but spread over two years, with mostly tax reductions now and less than a third of the total for public works and employment projects next year, after there has been time to design them.

To many, this represents timidity on all counts. But what has been slighted in the various analyses is the giant Carter ambition that lurks in this strategy. In sum, the President wants the means to lead, not just to preside, and who can blame him?

Scrap a tax: dodge an abyss

There seem to be four theories with which to greet the New Year. One must be dismissed out of hand, since it is only advanced by Cabinet Ministers and a few of our more gullible industrialists, namely that everything is pretty much all right and if only the Press would stop carping a new golden age is about to dawn. Nor is there much more evidence for a second, which seduces rather more people, that we may be declining but if we stay cool we can enjoy it. The scramble to unload the burdens of unemployment, inflation and general squalor on to somebody else's shoulders is already undignified, soon nasty, with an outside world too, whose willingness to feed and finance these introspective islanders can hardly be taken indefinitely for granted.

The weight of evidence really falls behind the third, that the decline is already so totally out of control as to be quite unstoppable, that we are seeing only the inevitable culmination of economic inadequacy, that it reflects deep-seated social psychological traits that connot be put right, that obstacles to corrective action are insurmountable. This is the case for emigration, for going off where hard work is still rewarded, and it is stunningly true that one meets far more successful, prosperous and contented British-born people abroad than ever at home.

So just for once let me try to be a little creative. Of course, there is no panacea, no one thing or list of things which if implemented would put it right. But nor is the situation so hopelessly confused that the general lines to which any successful strategy must conform cannot be identified. I read so many detailed analyses that all sound so totally different, yet in the end I think they are describing the same phenomenon.

No confidence in future inside EEC, Mr. Shore says

"Three years ago, on January 21, 1972, the Treaty of Accession to the EEC was signed. It carried the personal signature of Mr. Heath but emphatically not the endorsement of the British people. Incredible as it may now seem, neither Parliament nor people were privileged to see, let alone to debate the content of the crucially important treaty before it was signed."

Dealing with the econmic balance sheet of Britain's membership, he asked:

"Has membership brought that significant strengthening of the British economy which the advocates of entry so insistently proclaimed?

Unhappily, the balance of our trade with the EEC has tilted massively to the disadvantage of the United Kingdom.

It is no good for apologists to say that our trade gap has widened equally with all other markets. It has not. Apart from the special and uncontrollable deficit that has arisen this year with our oil suppliers, the great bulk of our nonoil deficit is now accounted for by our trade imbalance with the EEC.

Just why it should have developed so disastrously is not easy to answer. But no one should blink the fact that the "conventional wisdom", about the advantages to our trade of Common Market membership has been shown to be disastrously wrong.

Nor, unhappily, can we point to approaching improvements. It would indeed be a comfort if, in spite of our present appalling trade deficit, it could at least be shown that British industry, encouraged by the prospect of so large a tariff-free area, had embarked upon a major investment programme from which we would expect to benefit in one or two years' time. On the contrary, British industry, which had persistently clamoured for Common Market membership, greeted the event not with an expansion but with a massive curtailment of its investment plan."

Problems of re-cycling

Rubbish tips and scrap heaps are our only growing metal resource. By recycling one can obtain raw materials from native sources instead of straining the balance of payments further to pay for virgin material from abroad. Copper, lead, zinc and countless "tin" cans are lost in refuse tips annually. More serious still, effluent sludges of metal salts used in plating are responsible for the loss on an estimated 600 tons of nickel annually. Once dumped, these sludges may also be potential pollutants of ground water.

Considerable technological advances have been made towards separating closely intermingled metals in autos, alloys, appliances and the like. Shattering metal embrittled by refrigeration can facilitate separation; the less malleable will shatter into finer particles than those that remain more malleable.

As quantities of refuse continue to rise convenient sites for tipping and landfill are proving harder to find. Substitution of incineration for tipping could facilitate retrieval of metals, but vast quantities of valuable paper fibre and plastics would go up in flames.

A serious constraint on increased reclamation of paper fibres is the difficulty of finding wastes sufficiently uncontaminated to pulp.

Plastics are the most obstinately enduring of wastes. Much attention has been given to making them bio-degradable – whether by building light sensitive weaklinks into their molecular structure to allow sunshine to divide them into bite sized morsels of microbes, or by other means. Plastics fabricated of two or more compounds and those made via irreversible chemical processes cannot be remoulded.

Another route to recycling synthetic polymers is to release their energy potential. They are, after all, petroleum derivatives. Pyrolysis procedures reduce these compounds to fuel oil and waxes, something not to be scoffed at in these fuel-scarce days. Pyrolysis is a new twist on destructive distillation and involves heating materials in the absence of air.

Towards better control of environment

Glass that can help counter the sun's heat, insulate a roof, clear mist from a rear wind-screen, withstand bird impact at several miles an hour - these are some of the many functions now extending the versatility of glass and stretching the ingenuity of the manufacturer.

Pilkington, for example, has set up an environmental advisory service - part of a technical advisory service staffed with engineers, physicists and experts from other scientific disciplines - to aid the building team to integrate glass design with that of other building components and services. Such viability studies are part of this service. Pilkington's environmental service is now recognised as an unbiased consultancy with the objective of ensuring that optimum use of glass is made.

The computer, too, is being harnessed to problems of environmental control. Computer programs now available can determine the precise effect of any building component on internal thermal environment. They will provide "instant" cooling loads for any building in any latitude or orientation. More important, they will allow a finer analysis of the thermal contribution attributable to any individual building component. Through this service, precise predictions of air-conditioning plant size and cost for any combination of components can now be made.

Environment, particularly the safety aspect, is taken as seriously in the transport industry as in building. The latest development is a process for producing electrically heated toughened car rear windows which will demist on the inside and assist in de-frosting and de-icing the outside. A circuit, which is a series of equally spaced horizontal lines connected at the side of the glass by bus bars, is silkscreen printed on to the inside of the glass. The glass is then toughened, and the circuit is copper plated and finally nickel plated. Connections are then soldered on to the bus bars for wiring into the car's electrical system.

II
Übersetzung in die Fremdsprache

Wir erlauben uns, Ihnen die neueste Entwicklung unserer Forschungsabteilung vorzustellen, die einen grundlegenden Wandel im Maschinenbau bedeuten wird. Es handelt sich um einen Motor, der ursprünglich nur für den Einbau in Kraftfahrzeugen geplant war und an dem sich die Autoindustrie inzwischen auch schon sehr interessiert zeigt, obwohl für einen wirtschaftlichen Einsatz noch das Problem des zu hohen Gewichts gelöst werden muß. Die Versuche haben aber gezeigt, daß mit dem Einsatz in der Autoindustrie die Möglichkeiten dieses Motors noch lange nicht ausgeschöpft sind. Wir sind inzwischen in der Lage, einen so PS-starken Motor herzustellen, daß er auch für starke Maschinen in der Produktion eingesetzt werden kann, wo das Gewicht von untergeordneter Bedeutung ist. Unser Motor hat unübertreffbare Vorteile. Erstens besteht er aus weniger Teilen als jeder andere uns bekannte Motor. Aufgrund seiner Unkompliziertheit sind auch der Verschleiß und damit die Wartungskosten geringer. Zweitens ist er benzinsparender als vergleichbare auf dem Markt befindliche Modelle. Das ist eine sicherlich nicht zu unterschätzende Kostenentlastung bei den explodierenden Benzinpreisen. Drittens begnügt er sich mit bleifreiem Benzin. Nachdem weitere staatliche Regelungen im Bereich der Einschränkung der Umweltverschmutzung zu erwarten sind, ersparen Sie sich mögliche spätere Umstellungskosten. Der vierte Vorteil unseres Motors liegt in der Tatsache, daß er unglaublich leise ist. Es ist kaum vorstellbar, daß in absehbarer Zeit Motoren produziert werden können, die eine geringere Lärmbelästigung verursachen. Damit Sie sich davon überzeugen können, daß unser Brief keine leeren Versprechungen enthält, laden wir Sie herzlich ein, mit dem Leiter unserer Forschungsabteilung einen persönlichen Termin zu vereinbaren, an dem Sie sich von der Richtigkeit unserer Behauptungen überzeugen können. Wir sind sicher: Sie werden begeistert sein und nicht zögern, sich für unser Produkt zu entscheiden.

Brief I

Wir entnahmen Ihre Adresse der jüngsten Ausgabe des vom Internationalen Lederverband regelmäßig verbreiteten Journals. Wegen derzeitig geplanter größerer Produktionssteigerungen haben wir einen äußerst großen Bedarf an modernen Produktionsanlagen für Schuhe aller Art. Um zu sehen, ob Sie für die Lieferung der gesamten, oder eines Teils der Ausstattung in Frage kommen, bitten wir Sie, uns einen Überblick über Ihr Produktionsprogramm zu verschaffen. Zum Angebotsvergleich benötigen wir zudem Ihre neueste Preisliste, den frühest möglichen Liefertermin und Ihre Liefer- und Zahlungsbedingungen.

Im Falle eines konkurrenzfähigen Preisangebots und bei Erfüllung unserer Erwartungen hinsichtlich der Ausstattung und Qualität Ihrer Maschinen können Sie mit einem bedeutenden Auftrag rechnen.

Da wir für die Erweiterung des Betriebs Subventionsprogramme der Regierung zur Arbeitsplatzbeschaffung ausnützen möchten, deren Zuteilung entsprechend der Reihenfolge des Antragseingangs erfolgt, bitten wir um möglichst schnelle und umfassende Antwort, die Sie bitte direkt an unseren Prokuristen, Herrn M. Müller, richten wollen.

Brief II

Sie beanstanden in Ihrer Mängelrüge, daß auf der gelieferten Palette sich zwei Kartons weniger als bestellt befanden. Deshalb haben Sie, nach Ihren Angaben, einen guten Kunden nicht fristgerecht beliefern können, der Sie deshalb mit Schadensersatzforderungen konfrontiert. Gleichzeitig bemängeln Sie die schlechte Qualität der Lieferung von vorgestern.

Hinsichtlich der Kartons sehen wir uns außerstande, diese Reklamation und die Übernahme der Kosten für die daraus resultierende Schadensersatzforderung anzuerkennen. Die Lieferung erfolgte bereits vor vierzehn Tagen, wie der Lieferschein eindeutig beweist. Sie hätten Zeit genug gehabt - und obendrein die rechtliche Verpflichtung - , diesen offensichtlichen Mangel zu rügen.

Was die Qualität der letzten Lieferung anbelangt, ist Ihr Brief inzwischen gegenstandslos geworden. Unmittelbar nachdem wir feststellten, daß eine Maschine nicht ordnungsgemäß arbeitete, haben wir den Empfängern der schon ausgelieferten fehlerhaften Ware angekündigt, daß wir die Produkte auf unsere Kosten sofort bei Ihnen abholen und gleichzeitig einwandfreie liefern. Das sollte heute geschehen sein.

Brief 1:

Sie haben mir am 25. April d. J. unter Zeugen zugesichert, 500 Flaschen Bocksbeutel "Escherndorfer Lump" des letztjährigen Jahrgangs zum Preis von 5,90 DM je Flasche innerhalb von vier Wochen nach Abfüllung zu liefern. Jetzt verweigern Sie die Lieferung zu diesem Preis, weil sich durch die Trockenheit und den damit verbundenen Minderertrag die Preise auf ungeahnt hohem Niveau eingependelt hätten. Es ist im täglichen Leben und ganz besonders im Geschäftsleben unerläßlich, daß man sich auf gegebene Versprechen verlassen kann.
Als Kaufmann wissen Sie sicher, daß Sie mit Ihrer damaligen Willenserklärung einen rechtlich bedeutsamen Antrag abgegeben haben, den ich rechtzeitig angenommen habe. Auf diese Weise ist ein zweiseitiges Rechtsgeschäft zustande gekommen. Dieser Vertrag gibt mir Anspruch auf Erfüllung. Sie hätten Ihr unternehmerisches Risiko durch eine Preisgleitklausel mindern können.
Ich fordere Sie deshalb auf, unverzüglich zu den vereinbarten Bedingungen zu liefern, sonst sehe ich mich gezwungen, rechtliche Hilfe in Anspruch zu nehmen. Ich weise Sie vorsorglich schon jetzt darauf hin, daß bei Nichterfüllung Schadenersatzansprüche auf Sie zukommen werden, da ich meinerseits terminliche Bindungen bezüglich der Ware eingegangen bin.

Brief 2:

Die Zwangsvollstreckung gegen den Schuldner hat aufgrund des beiliegenden Vollstreckungsbescheids vom 3. Mai d. J. und des ebenfalls beiliegenden Pfändungsprotokolls des Gerichtsvollziehers Pfleiderer vom 5. Juli d. J. zu einer Befriedigung des Gläubigers nicht geführt.
Ich beantrage deshalb, daß der Schuldner die eidesstattliche Versicherung leistet und ein Termin dafür angesetzt wird. Falls der Schuldner zum Termin nicht erscheint oder die Versicherung an Eides Statt verweigert, bitte ich um Erlaß eines Haftbefehls und um Zusendung einer Ausfertigung.
Falls der Schuldner innerhalb der letzten drei Jahre die eidesstattliche Versicherung geleistet hat, bitte ich, die Terminbestimmung zu unterlassen und mir die Anlagen dieses Antrags mit einer Abschrift des seinerzeit vom Schuldner beschworenen Vermögensverzeichnisses zurückzusenden.

Aufstellung der Forderung:

1. Hauptforderung	1.000,-- DM
2. Gerichtsvollzieherkosten	8,-- DM
3. Portoauslagen und Mahnkosten	20,-- DM
	1.028,-- DM

zuzüglich 5 v. H. Zinsen auf 1.000,-- DM seit dem 1. Oktober.

Brief 1:

Wir beziehen uns auf Ihr Schreiben vom 17. August. Bei Prüfung der Angelegenheit haben wir festgestellt, daß die mit M. S. "Queen" versandten Thermometer und Manometer als Maschinenteile aufgegeben wurden und keine Markierung auf den Kisten auf die Zerbrechlichkeit des Inhalts hinwies. Nach den Bedingungen des Konnossements befreit uns die unrichtige Angabe des Inhalts von Packstücken von jeglicher Haftung.
Angesichts der Tatsache, daß wir mit Ihnen schon seit vielen Jahren freundschaftlich zusammenarbeiten, möchten wir – obwohl wir rechtlich nicht zur Zahlung verpflichtet sind – unsere Bereitwilligkeit zeigen, Ihnen entgegenzukommen und vergüten Ihnen per Verrechnungsscheck die Hälfte des Betrages Ihrer Reklamation.

Brief 2:

Wir haben Ihre Frachtnotierung für 10 Kisten Druckereimaschinen vom 06.09. erhalten. Wir bitten Sie nun, diese 10 Kisten gemäß unseren nachstehend aufgeführten Verschiffungsanweisungen nach Montevideo abzufertigen. Die Maschinen werden in der ersten Oktoberwoche von der Herstellerfirma Faber & Schleicher, Offenbach, frachtfrei Hamburg angeliefert. Sie sind mit dem ersten direkten Dampfer nach Montevideo weiterzuleiten. Keine Umladung in europäischen oder südamerikanischen Häfen. Teilverladungen sind nicht gestattet.
Bitte erledigen Sie alle Exportformalitäten für uns schnell und gewissenhaft. Wir haben die Hersteller angewiesen, die Maschinen teilweise auseinanderzunehmen, um Schwerfrachtkosten zu vermeiden. Wir bitten Sie, die Firma Faber & Schleicher nochmals darauf hinzuweisen, daß alle Oberflächenteile der Maschinen gut eingefettet werden müssen, um Rost und Korrosion während des Transports zu vermeiden.
Die Konnossemente sind, in drei Originalen ausgestellt, per Luftpost an uns zu senden. Sie sind an unsere eigene Order aufzumachen.
Versicherung der Sendung brauchen Sie nicht vorzunehmen. Die Maschinen werden von uns aus versichert.
Sobald die Sendung von Hamburg abgegangen ist, telegrafieren Sie uns bitte den Namen des Schiffes und ungefähres Ankunftsdatum.
Für die richtige Ausfüllung der Konsulatsfaktura erfahren Sie alle Einzelheiten betreffs Gewichten und Maßen der Kisten, Einzel- und Gesamtwert der Sendung vom Lieferanten.
Wir verlassen uns darauf, daß Sie alles Notwendige tun werden, um unsere Interessen bestens wahrzunehmen.

Brief 1:

Wir bitten Sie, zu Gunsten der Firma Max Müller GmbH & Co., Hofer Straße 15 - 19, 7950 Biberach, ein unwiderrufliches Dokumentenakkreditiv über DM 45.000,-- zu eröffnen, das bei Vorlage folgender Dokumente zahlbar sein soll:
Faktura in doppelter Ausfertigung, Versicherungsschein, ausgestellt über den Fakturawert zuzüglich 10% und Kriegsrisiko deckend, voller Satz reiner Bordkonnossemente, an Order ausgestellt, blanko indossiert und mit dem Vermerk "Fracht bezahlt" versehen.
Das Akkreditiv soll am 15.10.19.. ungültig werden. Teilverschiffung ist nicht erlaubt.
Wir danken Ihnen schon jetzt für Ihre Bemühungen.

Brief 2:

Ihre Anfrage vom 15.07.19.. haben wir mit größtem Interesse zur Kenntnis genommen. Wir mußten aber leider feststellen, daß wir die von Ihnen gewünschten Waren nicht in der Qualität, die Sie offensichtlich voraussetzen, herstellen.
Zu Ihrer Information übersenden wir Ihnen Qualitätsmuster unserer Erzeugnisse und bitten Sie zu prüfen, ob diese nicht doch Ihren Ansprüchen genügen.
Sollte für Ihr Programm jedoch nur die von Ihnen geforderte Qualität in Frage kommen, so wären wir nach einer Anlaufzeit von etwa drei Monaten sicher in der Lage, auch diese Ausfertigung zu liefern. Das setzt jedoch, wie Sie sicher verstehen werden, voraus, daß Sie uns eine Mindestabnahme von 600 Stück garantieren. Wir wären aber auch bereit, einem Jahresabschluß in gleicher Höhe zuzustimmen, der dann in Teillieferungen von mindestens 100 Stück abgerufen werden kann.
Nehmen Sie die vereinbarte Stückzahl nicht voll ab, so wird der Preis berechnet, der sich für die tatsächlich gelieferte Menge ergibt, zuzüglich 10% Aufschlag auf den Rechnungsbetrag.
Was ein Angebot unsererseits anbelangt, so wären für die Preiskalkulation genaue Angaben über die vorgesehenen Abnahmemengen notwendig.
Sobald wir eine diesbezügliche Mitteilung Ihrerseits erhalten haben, können wir Ihnen unverzüglich ein detailliertes Angebot unterbreiten, das bei Überschreitung der Mindestabnahmemengen durchaus Sonderkonditionen beinhalten wird, vor allem auch dann, wenn sich herausstellen sollte, daß Sie an langfristigen Geschäftsbedingungen interessiert sind.

Brief 1:

Sie wählen gut, wenn Sie sich für unseren XAY-Automaten entscheiden. Bei diesem Kauf möchten wir Ihnen so weit wie möglich entgegenkommen. Sie haben mit unserem Vertreter am 21.02.19.. Sondervereinbarungen getroffen, die wir wie folgt bestätigen:
1. Sie erhalten auf den Angebotspreis von 35.860,-- DM einen Sondernachlaß von 4%.
2. Wenn Sie die Maschine bis 28. d. M. bestellen, liefern wir ausnahmsweise schon innerhalb von 4 Wochen.
3. Zahlung: Nach Erhalt der Maschine durch Bankakzept mit einer Laufzeit von 2 Monaten ab Rechnungsdatum.
Sie entschließen sich jetzt sicher zu einem Auftrag. Der leistungsfähige und robuste Automat bringt Ihnen ebenso wie allen bisherigen Beziehern viel Nutzen.

Brief 2:

Aufgrund der immer stärker werdenden Konkurrenz hat sich unsere Buchhandlung auf fremdsprachliche Bücher spezialisiert. Wie wir inzwischen feststellen konnten, bestand und besteht noch in diesem Bereich in unserer Stadt und ihrem Umkreis eine Marktlücke. Dies wird wahrscheinlich daran liegen, daß wir hier nicht nur die Universität haben mit ihren fremdsprachlichen Instituten, sondern auch eine Reihe von Fremdsprachenschulen, die sowohl Übersetzer als auch Dolmetscher ausbilden mit abschließender staatlicher Prüfung. Das Interesse der Schüler und Studenten geht offensichtlich über ihre gewählten Fachgebiete wie Wirtschaft, Politik u.ä. hinaus; denn die Nachfrage nach Unterhaltungsliteratur ist ebenfalls gestiegen, seit wir anfingen, Werbung für unsere Fremdsprachenabteilung zu treiben.
Und hiermit komme ich zum eigentlichen Anliegen meines Schreibens:
während wir aus Ihrem Land mit Fachbüchern zwar schleppend aber regelmäßig versorgt worden sind, kommen die bestellten Bücher, die angeforderten Angebote und die Neuerscheinungslisten aus dem Bereich der Unterhaltungsliteratur erst nach mehrmaligem Mahnen.
Ich habe Ihnen unsere Situation geschildert und möchte Sie bitten, unsere Bestellungen pünktlich zu erledigen und Angebote und Neuerscheinungslisten regelmäßig an uns zu senden.
Bitte denken Sie daran, daß wir dazu beitragen, Ihre Sprache und Kultur in unserem Land zu verbreiten.

Brief 1:

Mit großer Bestürzung haben wir Ihren Brief gelesen, in dem Sie uns ankündigen, daß Sie die probeweise Herstellung der neuartigen Neonröhren (LK 032 Ihres Verzeichnisses) einstellen wollen. Wir sind immer noch an der Übernahme dieser Leuchtstoffröhren außerordentlich interessiert; denn - wie die Nachfrageentwicklung seit Monaten zeigt - besteht bei unseren Kunden der Wunsch nach stoßsicheren, leistungsfähigen Spezialbirnen jeglicher Art. Dies sind Ansprüche, die Ihre neu entwickelten Leuchtstoffröhren voll erfüllen. Dabei nehmen unsere Kunden den entsprechend höheren Kaufpreis gern in Kauf. Sie sehen also, daß sich Ihre Versuchsstücke hier von Verkaufsbeginn an gut bewähren. Wir möchten Sie deshalb heute noch einmal bitten, daß Sie die volle Produktion doch aufnehmen.
Falls Sie dies tun, sind wir bereit, zunächst einen Posten von 3000 Stück fest zu übernehmen. Die Lieferung müßte allerdings bis zum 15. Januar 19.. erfolgen. Um uns die erste Lieferung zu sichern, bieten wir Ihnen an, einen Teil des Gesamtpreises im voraus zu zahlen, und zwar einen Betrag von mindestens 20.000,-- DM am 01. Oktober. Sollten Sie jedoch nicht bis zum 15. Januar liefern, so müßten wir von Ihnen den gezahlten Betrag mit 10% p.a. Zinsen zurückverlangen.
Wir möchten Sie übrigens noch darauf hinweisen, daß nach unseren Erfahrungen eine Erhöhung des Preises von 20,-- DM auf etwa 22,-- DM pro Stück den Absatz in keiner Weise schmälern würde. Wir verlassen uns darauf, daß Sie die Röhren wie bisher in hervorragender Qualität liefern.

Brief 2:

Seit dem 25. d.M. befinde ich mich auf einer größeren Geschäftsreise in Deutschland. Wie bereits angekündigt, treffe ich am 05. September bei Ihnen ein, um mit Ihnen die erforderliche Neufestsetzung unserer Lieferungs- und Zahlungsbedingungen zu vereinbaren.

Bei dieser persönlichen Aussprache möchte ich Sie bitten, mir zu erklären, warum Sie unsere letzte Lieferung am 30. August nicht angenommen haben, obwohl die Lieferung ordnungsgemäß erfolgte. Eine Reklamation dürfte doch ausgeschlossen sein.

Brief 1:

Am 04.01.19.. haben wir von Ihnen eine Rechnung über DM 12.450,--, fällig am 01.03.19.. erhalten. Leider sehen wir uns nicht in der Lage, zum Fälligkeitstermin zu zahlen, da einige unvorherzusehende Ereignisse eingetreten sind. Seit Wochen warten wir auf die Zahlungseingänge eines langjährigen und bisher stets in allen Dingen pünktlichen Kunden. Wenn wir gewußt hätten, daß die Zahlungsschwierigkeiten auf völlige Fehlinvestitionen im Ausland zurückzuführen sind und nicht - wie man uns immer versicherte - auf konjunkturbedingte schleppende Auftragseingänge, hätten wir uns auf formloses Aufschieben der Zahlungen nicht eingelassen. Jetzt läuft ein Vergleichsverfahren, bei dem wir nach den vorläufigen Informationen wahrscheinlich nur 40% unserer Forderungen erhalten. Dieses Vergleichsverfahren ist in ungefähr 6 Wochen abgeschlossen. Etwa zur gleichen Zeit erhalten wir höhere Summen auf Grund der Fälligkeit einer gewährten Hypothek, so daß damit zu rechnen ist, daß unsere augenblicklichen Liquiditätsschwierigkeiten in höchstens zwei Monaten gänzlich behoben sind. Deshalb bitten wir Sie um Ziehung eines Wechsels über die oben genannte Summe auf uns mit einer Laufzeit von 60 Tagen ...

Brief 2:

Ich komme gerade von meiner ersten Reise zu dem von Herrn Bürkle übernommenen Kundenkreis in Süddeutschland zurück. Überall wurde ich herzlich aufgenommen, und die Kunden gaben wiederholt ihrer Freude Ausdruck, daß die Übernahme des Vertretergebietes durch mich so schnell und reibungslos erfolgt ist.
Wegen des außergewöhnlichen guten Weihnachtsgeschäftes waren die Lager der Kunden fast überall vollständig geräumt; ihre Bestellungen waren deshalb wesentlich höher als üblich. Soweit es ging, habe ich versucht, die Kunden aus den Beständen des Auslieferungslagers in Stuttgart zu beliefern, wobei ich allerdings auch den "Eisernen Bestand" angreifen mußte. Ich bitte Sie deshalb, so schnell wie möglich die noch nicht erfüllten Verträge zu erfüllen.
Außerdem verlasse ich mich darauf, daß Sie - wie verabredet - die regelmäßige Lieferung an das Auslieferungslager um 100 Stück auf 1.200 Stück pro Monat erhöhen. Eine ausführliche Liste lege ich bei.

Brief 1:

Bei einem früheren Besuch unseres leitenden Ingenieurs haben Sie sich darüber beklagt, daß Sie keine Elektromotoren bekommen, die die Leistungsfähigkeit der bisherigen Typen bei gleichen Preisen überbieten. Wir haben die Anregung aufgegriffen, und seit Monaten laufen darüber Versuche. Es ist uns jetzt vollauf gelungen, diese Verbesserung der Leistungsfähigkeit zu erreichen.
Wir haben einen neuen Elektromotor mit hoher Tourenzahl entwickelt, der die Leistung der bisher auf den Markt gebrachten Motoren weit übertrifft. Zunächst werden drei Ausführungen geliefert, deren Größenverhältnisse, Leistungen und Preise Sie aus den beigefügten Listen entnehmen wollen. Diese Listen zeigen natürlich nur einen allgemeinen Überblick, der aber vertieft werden kann durch Ausprobieren der Motoren. Danach sind Sie von deren Güte bestimmt ebenso überzeugt wie wir.
Wir empfehlen Ihnen daher, die Neukonstruktion in Ihre Warenliste aufzunehmen, und sind zur Lieferung eines Motors zur Probe nach den beiliegenden Bedienungsvorschriften gern bereit. Selbstverständlich führen wir Ihnen die Arbeitsweise der Elektromotoren auch jederzeit in unseren Geschäftsräumen vor; denn wir wollen es vermeiden, nur leere Reklame zu machen.

Brief 2:

Wie ich vorgestern von einem Geschäftsfreund erfahren habe, ist gegen die Firma Adam & Co das Konkursverfahren eröffnet worden. Ich habe auf Bestellung der Firma Adam & Co Büromöbel geliefert. Dabei ist von mir das Eigentumsrecht an diesen Möbeln bis zur vollen Begleichung des Kaufpreises von 2.500,-- DM, womit sie im Rückstand ist, vorbehalten worden. Zum Beweis übersende ich Ihnen den Kaufvertrag mit diesen Bedingungen als Anlage in Fotokopie. Daraus dürfte zu entnehmen sein, daß die Möbel nicht zur Konkursmasse gehören. Ich bitte um deren Herausgabe.
Falls die Möbel von der Firma Adam & Co oder von Ihnen verkauft sein sollten, verlange ich entweder die Abtretung der Kaufpreisforderung unter Bekanntgabe der Anschrift des neuen Erwerbers oder die Herausgabe des Erlöses.

Brief 1:

Mehrere meiner Kunden in der Schweiz haben mir mitgeteilt, daß Sie in der letzten Zeit von meinem früheren Vertreter M. Nägeli, der seit dem 01.12. d.J. in Ihren Diensten steht, aufgesucht worden sind.
Herr Nägeli hat den Dienst bei mir völlig überraschend und ohne jede Kündigung aufgegeben. Wie jetzt nachweisbar feststeht, ist er zu diesem Vertragsbruch durch die Zusage erhöhter Provision von Ihrem Sohn überredet worden, so daß ich jetzt verstehe, warum Herr Nägeli die ihn treffende Vertragsstrafe nicht geschreckt hat. Wegen dieser unlauteren Wettbewerbsmaßnahme muß ich außer von Herrn Nägeli auch von Ihnen Schadenersatz fordern.
Meine Kunden teilen mir empört mit, daß Herr Nägeli bei seiner Werbung in ungehöriger Weise die Vorteile Ihres Unternehmens gegenüber dem meinigen hervorzuheben sucht. Ich verlange, diese Art der Werbung sofort einzustellen.
Ich bin bereit, die Angelegenheit außergerichtlich zu erledigen, wenn bis spätestens 23.12. d.J. eine befriedigende Erklärung zu beiden Forderungen bei mir eingeht.

Brief 2:

Ihren Brief vom 15. d.M. habe ich erhalten.
Über den Vorfall muß ich Ihnen einige Erklärungen abgeben. Ich kann Ihnen aber gleichzeitig versichern, daß ich über die Handlungsweise meines Sohnes tief empört bin.
Vom 01.Oktober bis zum 15. Dezember d.J. befand ich mich zur Kur im Ausland. Für diese Zeit hatte ich sämtliche Vollmachten auf meinen Sohn übertragen.
Nach meiner Rückkehr hörte ich, daß Herr Nägeli unsere Vertretung in der Schweiz übernommen habe. Über die näheren Umstände, wie er unser Mitarbeiter geworden ist, erfuhr ich erstmalig durch Ihren Brief.
Die Angelegenheit tut mir sehr leid. Ich möchte sie deshalb persönlich in einem Gespräch mit Ihnen regeln, wenn ich Mitte nächster Woche in München geschäftlich zu tun habe.
Ich hoffe, daß Sie mit meinem Besuch einverstanden sind und verbleibe

III
Übersetzung aus der Fremdsprache

Time to sell off British Telecom

One of the untidier loose ends left hanging after the Government's decision to liberalise the communications industry is British Telecom's future financing arrangements. The issue is said to have caused much headscratching by Whitehall civil servants already.

That British Telecom will need substantially more external funding in future years than is likely to be available under the Government's cash limits and public sector borrowing restrictions is not seriously in dispute. The organisation will have to invest heavily if it is to modernise its national network and compete effectively with private rivals.

The disagreement is over method. The Industry Department wants British Telecom to be allowed to issue bonds, whose value would be linked to its future growth, in return for subjecting itself to stricter Government monitoring. But the scheme has become bogged down in a complex circular argument with the Treasury which hinges on the degree of investment risk which the bonds would – or should – carry.

A compromise must be found soon if British Telecom is to avoid a cash squeeze next year. There is a strong case for adopting the approach it has taken to Cable and Wireless: that is, to sell to the public 50 per cent of British Telecom (minus one share, to ensure continued Government control).

The Treasury would receive a windfall of, say, £ 700m at a conservative guess, and British Telecom's performance would be subjected to the discipline of scrutiny by the financial markets, which ought to prod it into becoming more efficient.

Interest, Charges, and Assessments in Respect of Special Drawing Rights Rule T - 1

(a) Interest and charges in respect of special drawing rights shall accrue daily at the rate referred to in (b) below and shall be paid promptly as of the end of each financial year of the Fund. The accounts of each participant shall be credited with the excess of interest due over charges or debited with the excess of charges over the interest due. The accounts of holders that are not participants shall be credited with the interest due.

(b) The rate of interest on holdings of special drawing rights for each calendar quarter shall be four-fifth of the combined market interest rate as determined in (c) below, provided that the rate shall be rounded to the nearest 1/8 of 1 per cent.

(c) The combined market interest rate shall be the sum of the average yield or rate on each of the respective instruments listed below for the 15 business days preceding the last two business days of the last month before the calendar quarter for which interest is to be calculated, with each yield or rate multiplied by the number of units of the corresponding currency listed in Rule O-1 and the value in terms of the special drawing right of a unit of that currency as determined by the Fund under Rule O-2 (a) and (b). The yields and rates for this calculation are:

    Market yields for three-month U.S. Treasury bills
    Three-month interbank deposits rate in Germany
    Three-month interbank money rate against private paper in France
    Discount rate on the two-month (private) bills in Japan
    Market yields for three-month U.K. Treasury bills.

Convalescence starts to pay off

The Eurodollar bond market continued its convalescence last week and may now have reached a stage where a few faltering steps upwards and even a mild issue or two may once again be in order.

The cure to the excesses of late June, when an unprecedented fall in U.S. short-term interest rates prompted a frenzy of trading and issuing, has now gone quite a long way. The great issuing binge started at yields of 13 % after Easter and took them down to 9 3/4 %. Today a prime borrower would probably have to pay 11 1/2 % to protect the still-aching investment banks from a relapse.

The secondary market moved very little. There were no shocks to the market from the massive treasury funding arranged in New York. Short-term interest rates stabilised with the six-month Eurodollar rate closing at 10 5/8 %. Certainly, there was no repeat of the rise in rates which had jolted the market the week before.

One Eurodollar rate which did move upwards was the five-year rate. Some attributed this directly to the five-year paper for International Harves Morgan Stanley expressly excluded call provisions from this bond to attract banks into it, and many arbitraged comfortly between five-year euro-deposits and the bond yield.

The pound sterling remains very strong and euro-sterling bonds offer impressive long-term yields. The domestic tremors over the money supply figures released by the unlacing of the "corset" shook domestic investors but probably meant rather less to foreigners. Prices in the euro-sterling bond market bounced back at the week's end to repair most of the damage.

Advertisement

A delegation from the Society of Motor Manufacturers and Traders will be flying to Mexico soon to meet the Japanese Automobile Manufacturers' Association.

They intend to pressurise JAMA yet again in order to obtain restrictions, for the fifth successive year, that will perpetuate for Datsun UK and their 400 dealers difficulties with cash-flow problems, with levels of employment and with stock to supply customers in Britain.

Since 1975, other importers from France, Germany, the Communist Bloc and anywhere else have been laughing up their sleeves at the restrictions on Datsun and other Japanese manufacturers, and have been pouring cars freely into Britain.

As a result, imported cars now account for almost 60 % of the UK market instead of 30 % five years ago. And still, it is the Japanese who are used as a scapegoat, even though their market share has stuck rigidly around the 10 % - 11 % mark, while other imports have taken off like a rocket.

So, what mandate does the SMM & T have to go to Mexico this January?

They ignore completely that the policy of the former administration, to use Japan as a diversion for their economic problems, is no longer fashionable. We have a new Government and new policies in operation.
1. This Government has stated many times that they believe in free trade and in freedom of choice.
2. The Motor Agents' Association, which represents 19.000 garages in Britain thinks it is time to be realistic. That stance has been endorsed by a committee of members representing every make of car from Austin/Morris to Volkswagen.
3. Prominent Members of Parliament see the futility of the present situation.

Iran nationalises nearly all of its modern industry

Preliminary estimates of the total investment involved ran to over £ 500m ($ 1.1 bn), though the parlous state of the domestic economy must have substantially reduced the net value of shareholdings.

The widely expected move follows the takeover of banking and insurance last month. It raises the pressing question of whether the new regime has the managerial and financial expertise to run the companies which range from Iran National, the biggest vehicle manufacturer, to sugar refineries and vegetable oil plants.

Combined with the wide holdings of Government agencies prior to the revolution, especially in the so-called "mother industries", and the seizure of the assets of the former Royal Family, the effect of the past month's nationalisation measures is to leave only a relatively small portion of Iran's economy in private hands. The main beneficiary is the traditional bazaar community, which has always had close links with the clergy.

The announcement on the state radio yesterday said the business assets of 51 individual industrialists and families were being taken over. Most had fled the country before the revolution, but there are notable exceptions.

No mention was made of compensation and as the announcement coincided with the Iranian weekend, no Government officials were available for comment. The main industrial sectors taken over are vehicles, steel and other metals, mining, heavy engineering, downstream aspects of oil and petro-chemicals, building materials and consumer goods industries.

Foreign companies are affected primarily through their joint venture companies set up with the two biggest industrial houses.

As the dollar falls stock markets rise

There is still no straightforward explanation for the continued investor confidence in paper instruments, to judge by the buoyancy of world stock markets, at a time when currency markets are in such disarray. Yesterday the slide of the dollar went on unchecked, hardly helped by a further rise in Japan's reserves and the apparent admission of the Federal Reserve chairman that there was little to be done except look on with benign neglect.

Part of the answer, however, seems to lie in the fundamental attractions of many stock markets as economies hover between one deep recession and hopefully a slightly less severe downturn. Certainly this time international interest rates are not being called upon to even out short-term capital movements but the extent to which stock markets are performing this function is open to argument. And while gold reached another all-time high yesterday, trading on the Swiss and London markets has none of the desperate characteristics about it associated with the currency crisis of the early 1970s with turnover well below record levels. Hot money is certainly using gold as a refuge on the margin, but there seem to be at least as many sophisticated investors seeing opportunities in world stock markets in the hope that the Bremen and Bonn talks turn out to be something more than hot air and that some news on the European currency front will emerge to take some of the pressure off the dollar as a reserve currency.

Disappointment

It will be up to EEC heads of Government to form their own judgment on the trade concessions extracted from Japan. But set against the advance billing by the Commission the results look rather disappointing. Apparently, it was deliberately setting itself exaggerated objectives, many of which it could not achieve. In public, officials have stressed the need for a dramatic turn-round in Japan's trade surplus with the Community. But in private, they admit that structural economic constraints would make it impossible for even the most co-operative Japanese Government to produce the required correction. - Obviously, the Community would have liked the kind of detailed list of individual concessions wrung from Japan by Mr. Carter. From its failure to get it - despite the application of as much negotiating muscle as the Community could muster - it is fair to conclude that the Japanese regard the consequences of a serious falling-out with Washington more seriously than they view EEC threats of retaliation.

The powerless Commission cannot resort to counter-measures which its negotiators have warned could result from continued Japanese intransigence. Most European Governments are far too concerned about the growth of protectionist tendencies in the U.S. to risk taking drastic actions against Japan which would be bound to create serious repercussions.

For months, however, many points at issue have been settled, e.g. crises eased by import restrictions, complaints diffused, tough concerted measures taken against third country import competitions, tensions relieved etc. European attention has been distracted by the decline of the dollar. Beyond the destabilizing effect on the world monetary system, there are momentous signs that it gives U.S. exports a significant edge while posing a challenge to European exports.

Industrial growth must be based on investment which supports profitable design, innovation and marketing

In spite of the current success of incomes policy it is clear that foreign indebtedness and the reduction of the rate of inflation remain more difficult problems for Britain than for other industrialised nations. Most economic commentators look for the cause of this difference in Government fiscal or monetary policy, in excess public expenditure or in low productivity due to inadequate industrial investment and worker motivation. Low investment is itself often blamed on stop-go policies, although it has now been demonstrated that the fluctuations in British economic activity have been less rather than more, than those of other countries. A recent study has shown that neither this nor differences in industrial structure account for the differences in performance of British and German industry.

The conclusion is that - given a lower rate of Government expenditure, leaving resources available for investment while reducing the balance of payment deficit - steady growth could be maintained, investment and productivity would rise and real incomes could increase. There is, however, very little evidence on which to base such a conclusion and a good deal of evidence demonstrating that there are basic deficiencies in British industrial performance which higher investment and more co-operative workers will not in themselves remove. Industrial policy must come to grips with these fundamental problems if the country's basic economic strategy is to succeed.

If the British standard of living is to be maintained, let alone rise, our exports must keep abreast of our imports.

The West's Slow Growth

The United States' economic revival might mislead us into imagining a comparable resurgence throughout the industrial West. Sadly, the latest analysis of the 24-nation Organization for Economic Cooperation and Development finds the non-Communist North to be experiencing the slowest postwar recovery analogous to but not so deep as the depressed 1930s.

Unemployment has risen over the past year, despite a 5-per-cent average rate of increase in real GNP. By itself, this would not be alarming. The jobless rate tends to lag behind the upturn of the business cycle as workers return to the labor market faster than they can be rehired.

More disturbing is the evidence that the recovery is already flagging. Real growth in the "Western" industrial world is expected by the OECD to slacken. That would mean more unemployment and new social and political strains, especially in Western Europe.

With labor, business and political systems under such a strain, the pressures for protectionism are bound to intensify. As the OECD points out, the Common Market demand that Japan curb exports of autos and other products is tantamount to the adoption of import controls. Even the United States, where the expansion has been relatively rapid, is hearing louder calls for protection from some industries and unions.

It is essential that the strongest economies that are least hampered by inflation aim for faster growth with new policies of stimulation. Stable but faster growth by the Big Three would increase their demands for imports and thus help other nations to move forward.

Chancellor's IMF Speech

Mr. Healey noted that the meeting was being held with the world in a recession without precedent in scale or duration since that of the 1930s.

Perhaps the main lesson to be learnt from the experience of the last two years was the need for greater awareness of the growing interdependence of the national economies of the modern world. Mr. Healey said that prior to the IMF meeting he had had discussions with his colleagues of the EEC in Venice and with his Commonwealth colleagues in Guyana. At both meetings it had emerged manifestly that recovery in the industrial countries was threatened if their trade with the developing world collapsed and that the developing countries were unable to avoid catastrophe unless the industrial world achieved recovery.

Mr. Healey expounded that Britain's problems were insignificant compared with those of the developing countries. Theirs had been and remained a multiple affliction – their exports had fallen in volume and in value while their essential imports such as fuel, food and fertilisers had risen in price, i.e. the terms of trade had become conspicuously unfavourable.

Mr. Healey hoped that the countries of the OECD as a whole would give serious attention to the explicit plea by Mr. McNamara that they should devote at least some small part of their incremental income to official development assistance. This applied particularly to those countries which had fallen behind to the others in their aid performance but would soon be enjoying the benefits of economic recovery. Moreover, both industrial and oil-exporting countries had to ensure that the concessional aid provided was directed primarily to those in exigency.

IV
Aufsatz

Themen zur Wahl:

1. The Japanese challenge: The background and the economic effects.
2. Job - sharing: advantages and disadvantages.
   (Annotation: one full-time job is split between two people)
3. What are the prerequisites for a hard currency? Give topical examples.

Themen zur Wahl:

1. More and better public transport systems, fewer private cars? Discuss the economic aspects.
2. What is inflation and in what ways can it be combated?
3. Comment on the following statement:
   "The two polarised viewpoints that economic prosperity and social progress come from either private ownership or state ownership alone are absurd". (David Owen, Labour Party)

Themen zur Wahl:

1. World Trade and the Dollar Crisis
2. The Problems of the Motor Industries in Europe and the USA
3. Steps taken by the industrialized nations and international institutions to relieve the Third World of its crucial economic situation

---

Themen zur Wahl:

1. What will change in Britain after the Government's White Paper on "The Government's Expenditure Plans 1978-79 to 1981-82"?
2. Agriculture and the EEC: What are the problems and how can they be solved?
3. In what way does the U.S.A. influence Europe's economies?

Themen zur Wahl:

1. Britain's bad economic situation: What are the reasons?
2. Concerns are growing bigger and bigger: What are the reasons and what will the future bring?
3. Is there a real up-swing in the U.S.A. despite the dollar crisis?

Themen zur Wahl:

1. West Germany's upswing in danger?
2. Will the international financial aids pull Great Britain out of her recession?
3. The dangers of a unified oil price, and the energy problems the industrialized nations have to cope with

Themen zur Wahl:

1. Compare the goals and methods used by trade unions in Great Britain, the U.S.A. and West Germany
2. New aspects of the EEC's relations with the rest of the world
3. Problems arising from economic growth

Themen zur Wahl:

1. Turkey, Greece, Spain, Portugal – Four new members of the EEC?
2. Price-fixing in the petrol retail trade – Pros and cons
3. Unemployed school leavers: Reasons – tendencies – solutions

Themen zur Wahl:

1. The impact of oil countries policies on the world economy
2. Problems of East-West Trading
3. The British White Paper "The Attack on Inflation" - Measures of the British Government against inflation and unemployment

---

Themen zur Wahl:

1. What are the pros and cons for Britain's continuing membership of the EEC?
2. The problems of recycling petrodollars
3. Changing the international monetary system. Which ways are possible?

Themen zur Wahl:

1. World-wide inflation and how to combat it
2. The economic situation of the U.S.A.
3. What's wrong with developing aid?

Themen zur Wahl:

1. The problem of the generation gap in management
2. The economic and social issues arising from foreign workers in Germany
3. The depletion of mineral resources and its effects on third world countries

V
Geschäftsbriefserie

Beteiligte:
Deutsche Firma: Schubert und Schubert; Frankfurt/Main
Ausl. Firma: G. Ball, London

Vorgang:
Die deutsche Firma testet seit kurzem die Möglichkeit der Einführung eines neuen Produktes der englischen Firma.

Aufgabe:
Erstellen Sie drei Briefe. Verwenden Sie alle notwendigen betriebswirtschaftlichen und rechtlichen Begriffe.

Brief 1:
Englische Firma informiert die deutsche über sehr angespannte finanzielle Situation (nennen Sie mehrere Gründe). Müsse deshalb ihr Produktionsprogramm vorübergehend auf wenige sehr ertragreiche Produkte beschränken. Deshalb werde keine weitere Lieferung der probeweise hergestellten Leuchter mehr erfolgen können. Bittet um Verständnis; sieht aber keine andere Möglichkeit.

Brief 2:
Deutsche Firma ist bestürzt. In letzten Wochen eine Reihe von absatzfördernden Maßnahmen eingeleitet (Beispiele), die sehr erfolgversprechend sind. Markt werde wohl einiges aufnehmen können. Möchte auf jeden Fall Weiterlieferung erreichen. Macht mehrere Vorschläge, der englischen Firma unter die Arme zu greifen, da eigene Liquiditäts- und Absatzlage zufriedenstellend. Müsse sich anderen Lieferanten suchen bei Einstellung der Lieferung. Könne deshalb bei späterer Wiederaufnahme der Produktion in der englischen Firma keine Abnahme mehr garantieren.

Brief 3:
Englische Firma geht auf Vorschläge ein. Hofft, besonders mit Hilfe der Absatzgarantien und der vorgeschlagenen Zahlungsbedingungen die eigenen momentanen Schwierigkeiten überwinden zu können. Großes Interesse, deutsche Firma als Kunden zu behalten (Gründe!). Dankt für großes Verständnis und Hilfsbereitschaft. Verspricht hervorragende Qualität und bevorzugte Belieferung.

Beteiligte:
Deutsche Firma: Schubert und Schubert; Frankfurt/Main
Ausl. Firma: G. Ball, Bandung, Indonesien

Vorgang:
Die ausländische Firma hat seit kurzem die Generalvertretung für die deutsche Düngemittelfirma.

Aufgabe:
Erstellen Sie drei Briefe. Verwenden Sie alle notwendigen betriebswirtschaftlichen und rechtlichen Begriffe.

Brief 1:
Die deutsche Firma ist verwundert darüber, daß die Umsatzzahlen weit hinter den Erwartungen zurückgeblieben sind. Man fordert einen sofortigen Bericht über die Ursachen an. Für den Fall, daß die Konkurrenz sehr stark sei, fügt man zusätzliches Prospektmaterial und Werbefilme bei, um auf dem Markt besser Fuß zu fassen.

Brief 2:
Von der Generalvertretung kommt die Antwort, daß die Qualität der Düngemittel hervorragend ankomme. Allerdings eine dringende Bitte: für eine bessere Verpackung der Produkte zu sorgen, da die Düngemittel durch die hohe Luftfeuchtigkeit leicht klumpen.
Eigentliche Ursache sind große Überschwemmungen. Durch die Schäden große finanzielle Schwierigkeiten der Reisbauern. Bitte um die Möglichkeit der Verlängerung des Zahlungsziels bei Verkauf an Reisbauvereinigungen, bei denen sich die Reisbauern – ähnlich wie bei deutschen Genossenschaften – ihrerseits eindecken.

Brief 3:
Die deutsche Firma weist darauf hin, daß den Düngemittelproduzenten in Deutschland der Wind stärker ins Gesicht wehe. Grund: Zunehmende Beunruhigung der Öffentlichkeit als Folge von wissenschaftlichen Veröffentlichungen über Rückstände in Nahrungsmitteln und deren Nebenwirkungen. Trotz eigener Schwierigkeiten habe man das Ziel, verstärkte Bemühungen außerhalb Europas und der USA zu unternehmen, um langfristig die Arbeitsplätze und die Rendite zu sichern. Angebot, jede erdenkliche Hilfe zu gewähren, natürlich auch die Zielverlängerung.
Hinweise bezüglich der landesspezifischen Marktsituation erbitten.

Beteiligte:
Deutsche Firma: H. Wild, Stuttgart
Ausländ. Firma: G. Ball, London

Vorgang:

Zwischen der deutschen Firma und der ausländischen Firma ist ein Kaufvertrag über 4 Maschinen zustande gekommen. Die deutsche Firma hat die 4 Maschinen zum fest vereinbarten Termin (15.01.19..) versandt, jedoch vergessen, den Versand der ausl. Firma anzuzeigen. Beim Verladen der Waren kommt es im Hafen Hamburg zu Verwechslungen, so daß die Maschinen den Bestimmungshafen nicht erreichen.

Aufgabe:

Fertigen Sie drei Geschäftsbriefe an. Verwenden Sie alle notwendigen betriebswirtschaftlichen und rechtlichen Begriffe.

Brief 1:

Die ausl. Firma schreibt an die deutsche Firma, daß die 4 Maschinen noch nicht geliefert sind. Sie drückt ihre Verwunderung aus, da sie die deutsche Firma als ausgesprochen zuverlässig kennt. Da die Kunden der ausl. Firma die Maschinen dringend brauchen, bittet sie, die Maschinen bis zum 20.02.19.. zu liefern, ansonsten würde sie von ihren Rechten aus dem Lieferungsverzug Gebrauch machen (entscheiden Sie sich für ein Recht, das Ihnen am geeignetsten erscheint).

Brief 2:

Die deutsche Firma schreibt, daß sie die Maschinen termingerecht versandt hat und bedauert, daß sie vergessen hat, den Versand anzuzeigen. Sie legt die Kopien der Versandpapiere und der Frachtbriefe bei und macht darauf aufmerksam, daß in diesem Fall kein Lieferungsverzug vorliegt (geben Sie die rechtliche Begründung dazu). Inzwischen hat sich die deutsche Firma erkundigt, warum die Maschinen noch nicht eingetroffen sind. Sie hat festgestellt, daß die Maschinen ordnungsgemäß in Hamburg angekommen sind, verladen wurden und daß dann jede Spur fehlt. Sie bittet deshalb die ausl. Firma, im Bestimmungshafen Nachforschungen anzustellen.

Brief 3:

Die ausl. Firma schreibt, daß sie festellen konnte, daß die Maschinen beim Verladen in Hamburg mit anderen verwechselt wurden. Es wird noch mindestens 12 Wochen dauern, ehe sie den Bestimmungsort erreichen. Die ausl. Firma bittet deshalb, so schnell wie möglich noch einmal 4 Maschinen zu schicken, da die Kunden drängen. Sie bedauert, daß sie zuerst angenommen hat, daß ein Verschulden bei der deutschen Firma vorliegt und hofft auf weitere gute Zusammenarbeit.

Beteiligte:

Deutscher Vertreter: Hans Wild, München
Ausländische Firma: John Ball, London

Vorgang:

Die ausländische Firma hat von einem ihrer Kunden, der Firma Otto Mylius, Essen, einen Brief erhalten, daß er in augenblicklichen Zahlungsschwierigkeiten ist, die ausstehenden 8.500,-- DM nicht zahlen kann und um "Stundung bis auf weiteres" bittet. Der Brief enthält keine Begründung für die Zahlungsschwierigkeiten und seine Angaben sind reichlich ungenau.

Aufgabe:

Fertigen Sie drei Briefe unter Verwendung der rechtlichen und betriebswirtschaftlichen Begriffe an.

Brief 1:

Die ausländische Firma schickt eine Fotokopie des Briefes des Kunden an ihren deutschen Vertreter und bittet um Nachforschungen; denn die ausländische Firma ist der allgemeinen Wirtschaftslage entsprechend in einer angespannten Liquiditätslage und hatte fest mit dem Eingang des Postens gerechnet, da der Kunde bisher recht zuverlässig war.

Brief 2:

Der deutsche Vertreter berichtet, der Kunde habe - wie erst jetzt bekannt wurde - bereits vor einiger Zeit bei fünf seiner Gläubiger um einen außergerichtlichen Vergleich gebeten. Zwei der Gläubiger gingen auf den Vergleich ein, was die finanzielle Lage nicht verbesserte. Inzwischen haben die drei anderen Gläubiger beim Amtsgericht Essen seinen Konkurs beantragt, da sie die Zahlungsschwierigkeiten glaubhaft machen konnten (geben Sie zwei Mittel der Glaubhaftmachung an!).

Brief 3:

Die ausländische Firma schreibt an den Vertreter:
1) daß mit gleicher Post ein Brief vom Amtsgericht Essen eingetroffen sei;
2) daß in vierzehn Tagen die erste Gläubigerversammlung in Essen, Humboldtstr. 23, stattfinden werde, an der der Vertreter teilnehmen soll (Vertretungsvollmacht liegt bei);
3) daß er ihre Forderungen beim Gericht anmelden solle (Liste der Forderungen liegt bei), damit die ausländische Firma in die Konkurstabelle eingetragen werden kann.

Beteiligte:
Deutsche Firma: M. Norten, Offenbach/Main
Ausländ. Firma: G. Brown, Edingburgh

Vorgang:

Zwischen der deutschen Maschinenfabrik und der ausländischen Firma ist ein Kaufvertrag über vier Spezialmaschinen zustande gekommen. Die ausländische Firma ist Zwischenhändler und hat die Maschinen bereits weiterverkauft an eine Firma, die sie für eine noch im Bau befindliche Fabrikhalle benötigt.

Aufgabe:

Fertigen Sie drei umfangreiche Briefe an. Verwenden Sie alle notwendigen betriebswirtschaftlichen und rechtlichen Begriffe.

Brief 1:

Die ausländische Firma bittet, die bestellten Maschinen pünktlich, falls möglich früher zu schicken, da der Neubau der Fabrikhalle des Kunden früher als erwartet fertiggestellt wird. Mit der Produktion könne bei vorzeitiger Lieferung sofort begonnen werden, was Vorteile für den Kunden hätte (Nennen Sie diese Vorteile!).

Brief 2:

Die deutsche Firma antwortet, daß die Maschinen einen Tag vor Eintreffen des Briefes bereits nach Hamburg geschickt worden sind. Inzwischen wird im Hamburger Hafen gestreikt. Die Dauer des Streiks ist ungewiß. Die deutsche Firma hat zufällig 6 Spezialmaschinen auf Lager, da ein anderer Kunde wegen Zahlungsschwierigkeiten vom Vertrag zurücktreten mußte. Die deutsche Firma fragt an, ob vier dieser Maschinen sofort per Luftfracht geschickt werden sollen. Dies würde allerdings Mehrkosten verursachen (Nennen Sie verschiedene Mehrkosten!). Außerdem besteht das Risiko, daß die bereits in Hamburg sich befindenden Maschinen nicht mehr zurückgehalten werden können.

Brief 3:

Die ausländische Firma stimmt der Luftfracht zu, da der Kunde die Mehrkosten übernehmen will (Nennen Sie Gründe für die Bereitwilligkeit des Kunden, diese Mehrkosten zu übernehmen!). Falls die Maschinen in Hamburg nicht zurückgehalten werden können, will die ausländische Firma diese in Kommission nehmen, da sie mit weiteren Aufträgen rechnen kann.

Beteiligte:
Deutsche Firma: M. Norten, Offenbach/Main
Ausländ. Firma: G. Brown, Edinburgh

Vorgang:

Die ausländische Firma hat in der Zeitung "Handelsblatt" eine Anzeige aufgegeben, in der sie für ihre Produkte (Folklore wie Röcke, Tücher, Teppiche etc.) eine Vertretung in Deutschland sucht.

Aufgabe:

Fertigen Sie drei umfangreiche Briefe an. Verwenden Sie alle notwendigen betriebswirtschaftlichen und rechtlichen Begriffe!

Brief 1:

Die deutsche Firma schreibt auf die Anzeige und bittet um Unterlagen (Kataloge, Preislisten etc.). Sie gibt an, wie sie sich eine Zusammenarbeit vorstellt. Sie nennt verschiedene Bedingungen, die in einem Vertrag aufzunehmen sind (nennen Sie diese Bedingungen). Die deutsche Firma gibt Referenzen an. Sie gibt auch Auskunft über ihre Tätigkeit und ihre Erfolge während der letzten zwei Jahre (beschreiben Sie sie).

Brief 2:

Die ausländische Firma schickt die gewünschten Kataloge etc. Sie ist mit einigen Bedingungen nicht einverstanden: die Kündigungsfrist müßte kürzer sein; eine Mindestabnahme müßte garantiert sein; die Wiederverkaufspreise müßten fest sein. Sie schickt den Entwurf eines Agentur-Vertrages mit den geänderten Angaben. (K E I N E N Vertrag anfertigen!)

Brief 3:

Die deutsche Firma ist mit den Vertragsbedingungen einverstanden, wenn bei Mehrabnahme als der festgelegten Mindestmenge sich die Provision erhöht (Staffelung der Provisionssätze). Sie bittet deshalb um eine Zusatzklausel im Vertrag.
Sie gibt ihrer Zuversicht Ausdruck, daß der Verkauf der Folkloreartikel gut anlaufen wird, da die allgemeine Modestimmung in Deutschland von Folklore bestimmt wird.

Beteiligte:

Deutsche Firma: M. Morten, Offenbach/Main
Ausländ. Firma: G. Brown, London

Vorgang:

Ein ausländischer Großhändler hat die Spielwarenmesse in Nürnberg besucht. Er ist von den Erzeugnissen der deutschen Firma begeistert und will einen größeren Posten Bausteine, verschiedene Puppen, Spielautos usw. kaufen.

Aufgabe:

Fertigen Sie drei umfangreiche Briefe an. Verwenden Sie alle notwendigen betriebswirtschaftlichen und rechtlichen Begriffe!

Brief 1:

Der ausländische Großhändler berichtet, daß er auf der Spielwarenmesse war und dort mit dem Vertreter der deutschen Firma gesprochen hat. Er wundert sich, daß die Preise überdurchschnittlich gestiegen sind. Trotzdem bestellt er lt. beiliegender Aufstellung Bausteine, Puppen, Spielautos usw., bittet aber um Preisnachlässe (nennen Sie sie!), deren genaue Höhe er angibt. Falls es keine direkten Preisnachlässe gibt, bittet er um Naturalrabatt.

Brief 2:

Die deutsche Firma lehnt höflich aber bestimmt ab zu liefern, da der ausländische Großhändler schon öfter bei ihr gekauft habe, aber unzuverlässig in der Bezahlung war. Die Rechnungen seien in der Regel erst nach mehrmaligen Mahnungen und ähnlichen Maßnahmen (nennen Sie mindestens zwei weitere Mahnungen!) bezahlt worden. So sei eine bereits 5 Jahre alte Rechnung überhaupt nicht ·beglichen worden. Dieser Betrag sei jedoch wegen der verhältnismäßig geringen Höhe bereits als uneinbringliche Forderung verbucht worden.

Brief 3:

Der ausländische Großhändler bedauert seine unpünktliche Zahlungsweise und gibt verschiedene Gründe (nennen Sie sie!) an, die alle außerhalb seiner Einflußnahme lagen. Er weist darauf hin, daß er diese Gründe bereits früher angegeben hatte. Zwar sei die noch nicht bezahlte Rechnung inzwischen verjährt, aber da sich seine Geschäftslage inzwischen stark verbessert habe, wolle er die erwähnte Rechnung trotz des nicht mehr bestehenden einklagbaren Anspruchs in den nächsten Tagen bezahlen.
Er kommt auf Brief 1 zurück und damit auf die Bestellung und bietet als Sicherheit verschiedene Möglichkeiten (nennen Sie alle Ihnen bekannten Möglichkeiten!).

Beteiligte:
Deutsche Firma: H. Wild, München
Ausländ. Firma: G. Ball, London

Vorgang:

Eine deutsche Unternehmung, die Ski und Rodelschlitten herstellt, hat von einem Geschäftsfreund gehört, daß die ausländische Firma gern die Produkte in ihr Programm aufnehmen möchte.

Aufgabe:

Fertigen Sie drei Briefe unter Verwendung der rechtlichen und betriebswirtschaftlichen Begriffe an.

Brief 1:

Schreiben Sie einen Brief an die ausländische Firma, in dem Sie sich erfreut zeigen an deren Interesse und daß Sie sie gern beliefern wollen. Machen Sie höchst genaue Angaben über die wesentlichen Bestandteile eines Angebots: z.B. Lieferungs- und Zahlungsbedingungen, Erfüllungsort, Gerichtsstand, Eigentumsvorbehalt usw. usw.
Aus Kostenersparnis schicken Sie ausführliches Informationsmaterial über die Produkte mit getrennter Post.

Brief 2:

Die ausländische Firma bestellt 100 Paar Skier und 100 Schlitten. Gleichzeitig möchte sie die Angebotsbedingungen ändern: leichteres Verpackungsmaterial wegen der hohen Transportkosten, höheren Skonto und sofortige Lieferung (Angabe von Gründen!).

Brief 3:

Die deutsche Firma erklärt sich mit dem höheren Skonto einverstanden. Das Verpackungsmaterial kann nicht geändert werden (Angabe von Gründen!). Kürzung der Lieferzeit auch nicht möglich, Vorschlag: Teillieferung; denn in den nächsten acht Tagen können 30 Paar Skier und 20 Schlitten abgeschickt werden.

Beteiligte:

Deutsche Firma: Reichert & Söhne, Düsseldorf
Englische Firma: Bennet Bros., Eastham

Vorgang:

Die deutsche Firma hat an ihren englischen Kunden Maschinenteile geliefert. Bei Übergabe der Dokumente hat der Kunde einen Wechsel in der englischen Währung über umgerechnet DM 2.000,-- (Angabe des Betrags) akzeptiert. Nun erfährt die deutsche Firma von ihrer Bank, daß der Wechsel nicht eingelöst wurde.

Aufgabe:

Fertigen Sie drei Briefe unter Verwendung der notwendigen betriebswirtschaftlichen und rechtlichen Begriffe an.

Brief 1:

Die deutsche Firma teilt ihrem englischen Vertreter den Sachverhalt mit und bittet ihn, Erkundigungen einzuziehen. Sie macht Vorschläge über eine Regelung. Für alle Fälle erteilt sie ihrem Vertreter eine Vollmacht, den Rechnungsbetrag zuzüglich Kosten und Zinsen einzuziehen.

Brief 2:

Der englische Vertreter schreibt an den deutschen Exporteur, daß der Kunde seine Zahlungen eingestellt habe und sich um einen Vergleich bemühe (Auskünfte über die Lage). Der englische Vertreter rät, einem Zahlungsvergleich zuzustimmen, wenn der Kunde in der Gläubigerversammlung 40% anbieten sollte (Begründung!)

Brief 3:

Der englische Vertreter berichtet: In der Gläubigerversammlung kam es zu einem Vergleich (40%). Bedingungen: Rückzahlung der Forderungen innerhalb von 5 Jahren; Verzinsung von 8%; 2 Bürgen haften selbstschuldnerisch (Kreditwürdigkeit begründen); Vergleichsverwalter und Gläubigerausschuß sind bestellt.

Beteiligte:
Deutsche Firma: H. Wild GmbH, Stuttgart
Englische Firma: G. Ball, Wolverhampton

Vorgang:

Die englische Firma bewarb sich um Übernahme der Alleinvertretung. Der Schriftwechsel ergab, daß die deutsche Firma – noch Neuling in dem Geschäftszweig, aber trotzdem schon leistungsfähig – nicht abgeneigt ist, im fremden Lande Fuß zu fassen. Der branchekundige Engländer wurde aufgefordert, einen Rohentwurf für den Vertrag einzusenden. Dieser Entwurf ist eingetroffen.

Aufgabe:

Fertigen Sie drei umfangreiche Briefe an, Verwenden Sie alle notwendigen betriebswirtschaftlichen und rechtlichen Begriffe!

Brief 1:

Die deutsche Firma ist mit manchen Punkten nicht einverstanden. Sie glaubt, ihr voraussichtlicher Vertreter wolle alles etwas zu groß aufziehen. Sie ist lieber für ein vorsichtiges Hineintasten in den englischen Markt. Manche Punkte müssen noch präzisiert werden, z.B. Provisionshöhe, Konsignationslager, Miethöhe, Ausfallbürgschaft, Verkauf auf eigene Rechnung, Beibehaltung anderer Vertretungen usw. – Die deutsche Firma verlangt vor der endgültigen Entscheidung einen ausführlichen Marktbericht und eine allgemeine Übersicht über die Richtung, welche die englische Gesamtwirtschaft vielleicht einschlagen wird. Die Vorschau auf Absatzerwartungen muß genau erfolgen. Übernationale Probleme müssen mit einbezogen werden.

Brief 2:

Die englische Firma gibt einen umfangreichen Marktbericht mit der geforderten zergliederten Untersuchung in die zwischenstaatlichen Probleme der Wirtschaft und Politik nebst Ausblick auf die nächsten Jahre. Mit den vorgeschlagenen Bedingungen ist sie, bis auf die Provisionshöhe und die Übernahme der Unkosten, die noch zu präzisieren sind, einverstanden. Ein Fixum wäre ihr am liebsten. – Sie lädt einen maßgebenden Herrn der deutschen Firma nach England ein.

Brief 3:

Die deutsche Firma dankt und wird ihren Verkaufsdirektor nach England senden, um dort die Einzelheiten zu besprechen. Er hat Generalvollmacht.

Mündliche Prüfung

Prima-Vista-Texte

A Fine Kettle of Fish

West German Chancellor Helmut Schmidt glared across his delicate porcelain coffee cup at British Prime Minister Margaret Thatcher. "Never have I seen such an example of national selfishness," he said. "You have gone back on a gentlement's agreement. You have cheated us out of an accord." Unperturbed, Thatcher replied frostily: "I do not propose to give in to these pressures. You are the ones who are blocking agreement. I have my national interests to look after." The subject was fish.
Schmidt's attack on Thatcher was triggered by Britain's refusal to endorse a European fisheries agreement. Last May, Thatcher had promised to support that proposal. Instead, Britain blocked ratification of a fishing treaty between the EEC and Canada – threatening the livelihood of West German fishermen who traditionally fish the waters off the Canadian East coast. The British contended that the treaty could dump 20.000 tons of fish this year on the British market. At last week's meeting Thatcher constantly irritated her Common Market counterparts by her references to "my fish" and "my waters". Passions were raised even further when French President Valéry Giscard d'Estaing who is running for re-election this year, proclaimed that he would never give up France's fishing rights.

Praying for Oil

Denmark's best hope for rescuing itself from big trade deficits is finding more oil. Which is one reason why the Social Democrat government was so determined to end the 50-year concession, signed in 1962, which gave the AP Moeller group and its partners in the Dansk Undregrunds Consortium (Shell, Texaca and Socal) an exclusive right to search for hydrocarbons on shore or off the Danish coast.

The government threatened to change the concession by legislation - which produced a counter threat from Moeller of a huge claim for compensation for expropriation. The company finally agreed this month to relinquish 99 % of its concession area, but the 12.000 square kilometres it will retain will all be in the south-west corner of the Danish North Sea sector, where all finds so far have been made. The consortium will also retain the fields it has found so far.

The government now hopes to tempt other companies to apply for licences leading to much more intensive exploration. The terms will be much tougher than those under the 1962 concession. How much interest will there be from oil companies? The geological structures in the Danish area are all small, and the most promising of them have been explored already. But Denmark's consumption is low - so even small additional finds could greatly reduce dependence on imports.

Zimbabwe Gets 2 Billion Dollars in Aid

Zimbabwe is seeking a "single massive infusion" of foreign assistance - and last week the new African nation began getting it. In Salisbury, the Zimbabwe Conference of Reconstruction and Development drew representatives from 36 nations and a dozen international organizations who pledged 2 billion dollars in aid. Topping the donor's list were Britain with a three-year pledge of 282 million dollars and the USA for 225 million dollars and the European Economic Community for 192 million dollars. "We see this as a demonstration of our attachment to Zimbabwe and of our profound interest in its future," said Britain's Lord Soames. For Salisbury, the conference was a complete success. The funds raised equaled the amount the government had hoped for to finance roughly one-third of the total cost of the nation's new three-year development plan.

While Salisbury continued to win friends in the West, the nation's formerly cordial relations with neighboring South Africa were moving in the opposite direction. Pretoria announced that it is terminating a seventeen-year-old preferential trade agreement with Zimbabwe that had allowed relatively free trade between the two nations and preferential tariff treatment for a number of Zimbabwe's exports.

Chinese investors discover Australia

A Chinese lawyer from Singapore took a one-week vacation in Australia - and spent a million dollars buying up prime real estate. A Chinese publisher from Hong Kong bought a bank building in Sydney for roughly 4 million dollars - and rapidly converted it into a thriving Oriental restaurant. With the speed of a tropical typhoon, cash-rich Chinese from Manila to Kuala Lumpur have begun snapping up some of Australia's choicest property, ranging from hotels to shopping centers to industrial sites. And they are eagerly looking for more. "The boom conditions in Hong Kong and elsewhere have generated a lot of ready cash", says a Sydney real-estate consultant. "And it makes sense to spread more and more of the profits around."
The Chinese enthusiasm for Australian property springs from several sources. A boom in energy projects and mineral development in Western Australia, New South Wales and Victoria has spurred demand for increased housing. Australia also provides a nearby base for Chineseowned companies that have reached their domestic growth limits. And many Chinese hope that owning property in Australia will make it easier to emigrate there - though that idea is hotly denied by Australian immigration authorities. "It is not possible to buy one's way into Australia," says a senior government official. "Being an entrepreneur is just one condition in a long list of criteria for entry."

"Voluntary" Restrictions

The surge of Japanese auto imports into the USA has led to a growing pressure from top industry executives, government officials and legislators for "voluntary" restraints on the part of Japan. Even Roger Smith, the new chairman of General Motors Corp., the one automobile company that had consistently backed free trade in autos, has joined the clamor for voluntary restrictions.

Needless to say, the talk of voluntary restrictions is hypocrisy pure and simple. Japanese exporters are not about to cut their own throats "voluntarily". They will restrict exports only if their government requires them to do so - whether openly and explicitly or by more subtle means of persuasion. And the Japanese Government will require them to restrict exports only if our government pressures or bribes Japan to do so.

The feature of voluntary restrictions that appeals to the automobile industry is at the same time one of the strongest arguments against the measure: such restrictions can be negociated by Executive action; and opposition to them can be more easily muzzled and circumvented than opposition to legislated restrictions. In short, voluntary restrictions are a form of taxation without representation.

California's rotting shame

Even amid the groves of California's San Joaquin Valley, the sight is startling. Covering acre after acre, mounds of navel oranges lie rotting in the sun. This season's crop hit a record 1.421.250 tons, but nearly half of it will never reach the fresh-produce markets. The result: a large navel oranges costs as much as 70 cents in Chicago, up from 50 cents last year. The oranges are being dumped because of U.S. Department of Agriculture "marketing orders", regulations that limit sales of twelve varieties of farm-products. In the case of the navel oranges, an eleven-member committee, dominated by industry representatives, meets weekly in Los Angeles from November to June to decree how much fruit can be shipped from the groves. Most Florida oranges are used for juice and thus are exempt from the regulations. Anyway, the Florida crop has shrunk from last year's because of a midseason freeze.

Agriculture officials admit that the marketing orders prop up the price of oranges, but argue that the rules prevent gluts and shortages. Public interest groups take a different view. Charges Harry Snyder of Consumers Union: "It's a welfare system for farmers that denies cheap food for poor people." Not surprisingly, Vice President Bush last week put the orders on the Administration's hit list of 27 existing Government regulations that will be closely examined.

Pay up or Stay Home

Philadelphia's buses and underground system are paralysed by a strike, called because the authority wanted permission to hire part-time workers as 5 % of its labour force. But Philadelphia is comparatively lucky. Birmingham, Alabama, a city of 800.000 has no public transport at all; it was shut down because the city had run out of money for it. In Chicago the transport authority may be bankrupt by April 1st unless the state comes to the rescue. An 80-cent fare simply does not bring in enough revenue at a time when costs are soaring.
Other big cities, particularly those in the north-east and mid-west, are also struggling with deficits, complaints about delays and breakdowns, cuts in service, and fares that are higher than Americans are accustomed to pay. For all those reasons, and because the price of gasoline is still not prohibitive, the numbers of passengers on public transport have been falling, adding to the deficits. The census bureau reported recently that in 20 metropolitan areas (not including New York) only 7 % of workers used public transport in 1977 compared with over 10 % in 1970. More than 90 % of commuters still drove to work; 72 % carried no passengers. So much for conservation of imported oil and reduction of pollution.

Down Again

Laker Airways, leading the pack to push transatlantic fares up dramatically this month, has been the first to break ranks and push them down again to where they had started. Sir Freddie Laker called the price rise "a mistake".

Bookings had dropped sharply after the airlines announced new rates up to 50 % higher than before. Pan Am, TWA and British Airways have quickly followed Laker in putting their fares down again. If, as most airlines expect, Laker's next filing of new fares, announced on April 7th, proposes a new but more modest rise, they will presumably follow on up again.

But if the airlines do find they are stuck with low (or fairly low) prices for long, they will probably cut capacity on the North Atlantic quite sharply. They may abandon some less attractive routes (e. g. Boston-Europe, or Brussels and Amsterdam to America). And where does this about-turn leave Laker? It puts up fares so mightily because of the interest burden of its debt for a handsome fleet of new aircraft.

On the Economic Progress of Black America

The dangers of an analysis such as the one I have presented is that it does overemphasise the "good news". For example, the figure given at the beginning of this article that northern black couples under the age of 35 have essentially equalled the average income of their white counterparts is somewhat misleading. It is only true for black families in which both husbands and wives work. For those families in which only the husband works there was, relative to whites, no gain between 1959 and 1970. Moreover the harsh fact is that the centre of gravity of the blacks remains anchored in jobs requiring little skill and with little future. The heartland of northern black life is still the inner-city ghetto with its garbage-strewn streets, broken windows, and badly-lit alleys where crime is rampant and life insecure.

It is this environment - perpetuated by the high rates of unemployment, the still widespread discriminatory job practices, and an archaic and primitive welfare system - that is accounting for the visible deterioration of the habitat and the inhabitants of the big cities.

Steel War?

On steel, West Germany found itself in lonely isolation, pitted against other European producers. An agreement to cut back surplus production is due to run out in three months. If a new agreement to curb overproduction is not reached, a fratricidal steel war could break out between West Germany's efficient, privately run plants and the sluggish state – subsidized steel producers of most other EEC nations. At cne point Schmidt warned that Bonn might impose import taxes on steel from its EEC partners, an act that could summarily bring an end to the free circulation of iron and steel products in Western Europe. Again the problem was shunted aside to aides.

On the diplomatic front, the Europeans decided to remind Washington of the need to stick to the two-track approach to East-West relations that has been standard NATO policy since December 1979 – a determination to modernize nuclear weapons in Europe coupled with sincere efforts to negotiate with the Soviets on nuclear disarmament. At the end of the two-day meeting, there was a general agreement that little of substance had been achieved. But as Schmidt told West German reporters: "I'm not disappointed because I didn't expect anything to come of this." For the most part, he was right.

FACHVERLAG TH. GROSSMANN   Ebitzweg 18   7000 Stuttgart 50

ISBN	Fachbuchreihe „Der Weg zum guten Handels- und Wirtschaftsenglisch":
	Freyd-Wadham,
	Englisches Wirtschaftsalphabet
	(English Economic Terms with German Vocabulary)
3-87217-006-6	8. Auflage, 156 S., celloph. Umschlag

Grossmann/Freyd-Wadham,
Englisches Handelsvokabularium nach Sachgebieten
(mit Gesamtwortverzeichnis)
3-87217-001-5   5. Auflage, 330 S., celloph. Umschlag

Freyd-Wadham,
Englische Geschäftsbriefe
(Anleitung zur englischen Handelskorrespondenz)
3-87217-007-4   144 S., celloph. Umschlag

Freyd-Wadham/Grossmann,
Englische kaufmännische Übersetzungstexte
(mit deutschen Vokabeln und Erläuterungen,
mit engl. Übersetzungen der deutschen Texte in
„Engl. Geschäftsbriefe")
3-87217-008-6   120 S., celloph. Umschlag

Prüfungstexte für die fremdsprachliche Wirtschafts-korrespondentenprüfung
3-87217-160-7   Englisch, 72 S.
3-87217-170-4   Französisch, 80 S.

Grossmann-Friedmann,
Kaufmännisches Grundwörterbuch für Schule und Praxis
3-87217-300-6   Teil I   Deutsch—Englisch, 280 S., celloph. Umschlag
                Teil II Englisch—Deutsch, in Vorbereitung

Ziegler,
Grammatisches Wörterbuch der gebräuchlichsten spanischen Verben
mit Satzbeispielen, Konjugations- und Sondertabellen
3-87217-009-0   160 S., celloph. Umschlag

Grossmann,
Fachbücher für Fremdsprachenstenografie
(Anpassung der deutschen Einheitsstenografie):

English Shorthand
3-87217-020-1   Teil I   —   Verkehrsschrift (20. Aufl.)
3-87217-030-9   Schlüssel zum Teil I (für Selbstlernende)
3-87217-040-6   Teil II   —   Eilschrift (9. Aufl.)
3-87217-050-3   Schlüssel zum Teil II
3-87217-060-0   Teil III —   Lese- und Schreibübungen
3-87217-080-5   Taschenwörterbuch English Shorthand

Stenographie Française
3-87217-090-2   Teil I   —   Verkehrsschrift (5. Aufl.)
3-87217-091-0   Schlüssel zum Teil I
3-87217-092-9   Teil II   —   Eilschriftliches Wörterbuch

Taquigrafia Española
3-87217-095-3   Teil I   —   Verkehrsschrift (3. Aufl.)